Uncharted Territory

by Soham Milan Mody

Soham Mody

BookLeaf Publishing
India | USA | UK

Made with ❤ on the BookLeaf Publishing Platform
www.bookleafpub.in
www.bookleafpub.com

To my family…

Acknowledgements

This book represents not just a culmination of my work, but also a testament to the unwavering support and encouragement provided by numerous remarkable individuals along this journey.

First and foremost, I wish to extend my profound gratitude to my beloved parents, whose endless patience, unwavering support and deep belief in my potential have been my guiding light. Their inspiration has been invaluable, and their encouragement has played an irreplaceable role in my endeavours.

I would also like to express my sincere appreciation to BookLeaf Publishing for their invaluable insights, expert guidance and meticulous attention to detail throughout the process of shaping this manuscript. Their professionalism and commitment have significantly contributed to the successful realisation of this project, and for this, I am deeply grateful.

Lastly, I wish to acknowledge my esteemed readers. Thank you for choosing to engage with this book and for granting me the honour of sharing my story, thoughts and ideas. Your time, attention and interest are the most precious gifts I could ever hope to receive, and I am sincerely grateful for the opportunity to connect with you through these pages.

With heartfelt gratitude,

Soham

Foreword

It's been a delight watching Soham grow, from the little one I remember to the remarkable young man he is today. He has a natural gift with language, a real flair for shaping his thoughts and feelings into words that resonate. There's a lightness to his writing, a touch of humour that makes even the deeper themes feel accessible and engaging.

We all know how fleeting moments can be, how easily they slip through our fingers. Poetry, though, has this incredible power to capture a sliver of that feeling and enable us to hold onto something precious.

Soham's poems don't just rhyme; they dance on the page. They provoke thought, offer comfort and give us glimpses into his unique perspective. His imagination and intellect intertwine beautifully, and emotions find their form in carefully chosen words.

I'm thrilled to introduce you to Soham's debut collection. These poems have a way of staying with you long after you've finished reading. Let the magic begin!

All the best
Khurshed Batliwala

Khurshed Batliwala, affectionately known as "Bau," is a multifaceted individual with a diverse range of talents and passions. He holds an M.Sc. in Mathematics from the prestigious Indian Institute of Technology (IIT) Bombay.

Over 30 years ago, Khurshed decided that he would rather help people find inner peace and joy through meditation than teach them mathematics. He became a faculty member of the Art of Living.

In addition to his other pursuits, Khurshed is also an author. He has written several books on topics related to self-improvement, happiness, and meditation. His writing often blends his scientific background with spiritual insights, making complex concepts accessible to a wide audience. Some of his notable works include "Ready, Study, Go!: Smart Ways to Learn," "Sleep Your Way to Success," and "Happiness Express."

Preface

Welcome, to the adventurous pages of Uncharted Territory. Herein lies a collection of poems that traverse the often tumultuous landscape of life's hurdles. Each poem serves not merely as a reflection of our collective experiences but as a beacon of hope, illuminating the path through those winding, bumpy roads we all seem to travel.

Life, as we know, is a series of unpredictable events – an exquisite chaos that can sometimes feel like a clumsy dance in a crowded ballroom. You twirl gracefully for a moment, then suddenly step on a toe. And, oh, the shrieks! But fear not, for with a little practice (and perhaps some sturdy shoes), we can begin to navigate gracefully through the footsie of life.

When I first embarked on this poetic journey, I imagined each poem as a lifebuoy tossed out into the swell of uncertainty. Some may float, while others might sink like stones – but that's part of the fun, right? The goal is not perfection, but rather the pursuit of understanding and, dare I say, a good chuckle at the absurdities we face.

In the following verses, you will encounter the trials we all endure: the heartbreak of lost dreams, the struggle against self-doubt and the moments when it feels like the universe is playing an elaborate practical joke on us. These aren't just my hurdles; they are the hurdles of every human who has navigated the complicated terrain of existence. Consider this book a friendly compendium of knobby knees, scraped shins and some truly questionable life choices.

As you navigate through this jungle of rhymes, I encourage you to embrace the humour that life throws our way. The ability to laugh at ourselves in the face of adversity is more than just an admirable quality; it is a necessary survival tool! Think of it as a life preserver adorned with glitter. Its light-heartedness, when mixed with resilience, can lead us to powerful transformations. Yes, this book offers wisdom, but it offers laughter too – after all, who wouldn't want to chuckle their way through a series of existential crises?

Through poetry, I aim to explore the myriad ways we respond to life's challenges – sometimes with grace, but often with flailing limbs and face plants. Each poem acts as a small guide, urging you to embrace vulnerability and see it not as a sign of weakness but as an essential part of the journey. Whether you find yourself lost in a dense fog of confusion or skip along the sunny paths of enlightenment, these words are here to accompany you.

Don't be surprised if you find yourself laughing out loud, rolling your eyes or even shedding a tear or two; this rollercoaster is all part of the ride. Allow your heart to leap, stumble and occasionally trip over its shoelaces. These verses are the shoes I'm offering to you – sometimes sturdy, sometimes whimsical – designed to carry you forward, no matter how bumpy the road gets.

Each section of this book addresses a different hurdle we may encounter: love and loss, dreams and failures, joy and despair. I've deconstructed these experiences with a blend of sincerity and levity, hoping to spark moments of recognition and maybe even bring a smile to your face. I aim to offer both comfort and inspiration as we navigate life's unpredictable waters together.

By the end of your journey through this book, I hope that you will feel a little more equipped to face whatever life throws at you, or at least laugh heartily in its face. Remember, you're not alone in this – each of us is a traveller in this uncharted land, armed with nothing but bravery, charm and occasionally embarrassing stories. So, buckle up! Here's to embracing the unknown, turning hurdles into stepping stones and finding laughter along the way.

Thank you for joining me on this whimsical adventure. May you find solace, joy and a sprinkle of absurdity within these pages. Let's embrace the uncharted together, one poem at a time, and, if we're lucky, we just might discover treasures hidden within the hurdles of our shared human experience.

Welcome to Uncharted Territory.

Euphoria and Anguish

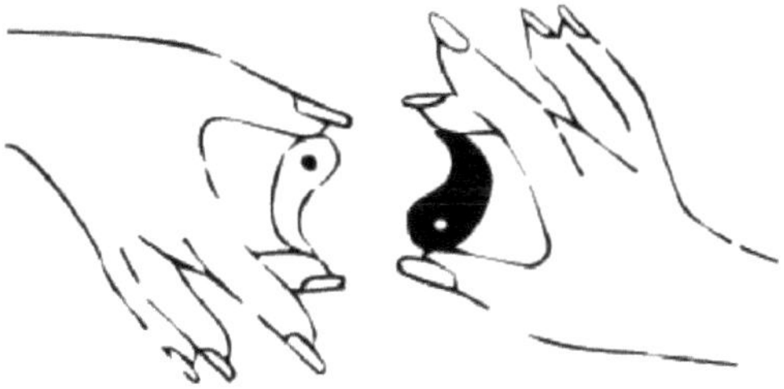

In the burst of morning light,
joy dances on the edges of dreams,
like laughter shared between friends,
filling the air with bright colours,
every heartbeat a promise,
every glance a story yet to unfold.

But behind the curtain, shadows linger,
heavy and dark, like a winter's chill,
clutching at the corners of a smile,
whispers of what could break.
Anguish waits, a silent thief,
stealing moments, dimming the glow.

We walk this tightrope,
balancing on the line of hope and fear,

the sweet taste of victory
suddenly tainted by the squeeze of loss.
A memory flickers like a dying flame,
its heat still warming the heart.

In laughter, we feel the weight of grief,
a smile that hides bruises beneath,
yet we rise, again and again,
wrapping ourselves in the light,
as if it were a shield against the night.

Euphoria and anguish,
two sides of the same coin,
we hold them close,
and learn to dance
to the songs they sing,
in this life of contradictions,
where joy and pain flow
like rivers, forever entwined.

Anger, Unchained

The storm inside, a raging sea,
A tempest brewing, wild and free.
The anger swells, a rising tide,
A force unleashed, a raging guide.

The world grows dim, a darkened sight,
The heart pounds fast, with all its might.
The mind is clouded, thoughts unclear,
The path ahead, a source of fear.

The words escape, a hurtful dart,
The pain inflicted, a wounded heart.
The tears well up, a silent cry,
The soul is weary, asking why.

The anger fades, a calming breath,
The storm subsides, a peaceful death.
The mind is clear, the heart is light,
The future beckons, shining bright.

But still, the echoes linger on,
A haunting memory, a shadow drawn.
The scars remain, a painful sight,
A reminder of the darkest night.

But from the ashes, hope will rise,
A phoenix soaring, towards the skies.
The past is gone, the future's clear,
A new beginning, drawing near.

The anger fades, a distant dream,
A fading memory, a fleeting gleam.
The heart is healed, the soul is free,
A new dawn breaks, eternally.

Jealousy's Sting

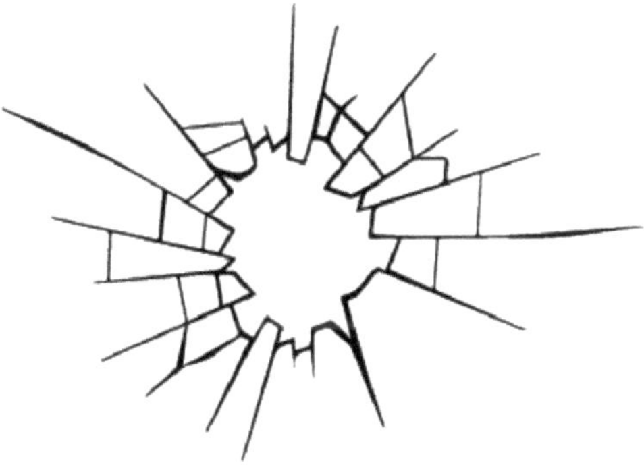

In shadows deep where whispers creep,
A serpent coils; its secrets keep.
With emerald eyes that pierce the night,
Jealousy stirs, a bitter blight.

It slithers close, a silent thief,
Sowing seeds of doubt and grief.
A heart once whole, now torn apart,
By envy's grip on the tender heart.

It watches love with hungry gaze,
Transforms sweet moments into haze.
A smile that glows, a laugh that sings,
Now tainted by what jealousy brings.

Like ivy creeping on a wall,
It wraps around; it seeks to sprawl.
The joy of others feels like pain,
As green-eyed spectres dance in vain.

Yet in this dark, a lesson lies:
To cherish love and cut the ties.
For trust can bloom where envy fades,
And light can break through shadowed
glades.

So let us cast away the sting,
Embrace the joy that friendship brings.
For in the heart where love is true,
There's room enough for me and you.

Regrets Echo

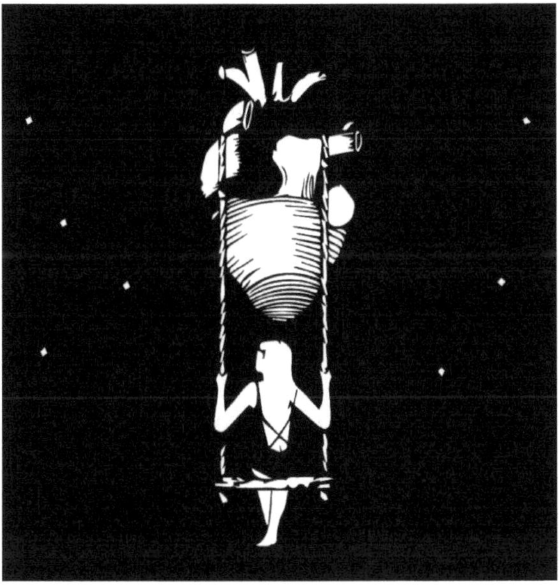

In the quiet chambers of the mind,
Where shadows dance and whispers bind,
Regrets like echoes softly creep,
In the stillness where memories sleep.

They flutter like leaves in autumn's breeze,
Carrying tales of what could have been,
Each choice a thread, each path a seam,
Woven into the fabric of dreams

A word unspoken, a chance passed by,
Moments that linger, like stars in the sky,
Their light may fade, but the shadows remain,
A haunting refrain of joy mixed with pain.

Oh, the roads not taken, the bridges burned,
Lessons unlearned and wisdom spurned,
Yet in this echo lies a gentle grace,
A chance to reflect, to slow down the pace.

For every regret is a story to tell,
A piece of our journey where we stumbled and fell;
Embrace the echoes; let them guide you through,
For in their soft whispers lies the strength to renew.

So let not regret be a weight on your heart,
But a map of your journey, each scar a fine art;
In the symphony of life, let each note resound–
For even in echoes, true wisdom is found.

Self-Doubt's Shadow

In the quiet chambers of my mind,
echoes of whispers linger,
sharp as shattered glass,
each word a dagger,
each thought a storm,
the relentless tide of self-doubt.

I stand at the edge of a mirror,
my reflection fractured,
a mosaic of failures and angst,
the weight of expectations,
heavy as a leaden sky,
pressing down on the fragile wings of hope.

‘Not enough,’ it hisses,
a serpent coiled around my heart,
‘Unworthy,’ it sneers,
a shadow that dances in the corners of my soul.
I wear these chains like a second skin,
the armour of inadequacy,
crafted by hands that know only how to criticise.

But in the stillness, a flicker ignites–
a whisper of something softer,
a voice that breaks through the cacophony:
‘You are more than your scars’.
And I pause, breath catching in my throat,
as the tendrils of compassion unfurl.

What if I could cradle my pain like a child?
What if I could hold each flaw with tenderness,
like petals trembling in the wind?
To breathe life into the shadows,
to paint them with colours of understanding–
the blues of sorrow, the greens of growth.

I gather the fragments of my spirit,
each piece a story waiting to be told:
the moments of laughter that danced in
sunlight,
the quiet victories that went unnoticed.
I weave them together with threads of
kindness,
stitching a tapestry rich with resilience.

In this new light, I see–
self-loathing is not a fortress but a prison.
I unlock the door with keys forged in
empathy,
step into the garden where wildflowers
bloom.
Here, I learn to nurture the soil of my heart,
to plant seeds of acceptance in every crack.

With each passing day, I cultivate grace–
the art of being human in all its messiness.
I embrace the imperfections that make me
whole,
the laughter that spills from tears uncried.
And as I walk this path towards self-love,
I find strength in vulnerability's embrace.

So let the shadows linger; they are part of me.
But now I dance with them – no longer
afraid.
In this sacred space where compassion reigns,
I rise from the ashes of my own making,
a phoenix wrapped in warmth and light.

Fear's Grip

In shadows deep, where whispers creep,
A silent foe begins to seep,
Through cracks of doubt, it weaves its thread,
A tapestry of thoughts unsaid.

It grips the heart with icy hands,
And builds its fortress on shifting sands.
Each breath a battle, each moment a fight,
As darkness dances, swallowing light.

The mind, a maze where phantoms play,
In corners dim, they twist and sway.
The future looms – a daunting spectre,
With every heartbeat, fear's protector.

Yet in the depths where shadows loom,
A flicker sparks – a chance to bloom.
For courage whispers in the night,
To face the fears and seek the light.

So let them come, those ghosts of dread,
With open arms, I'll forge ahead.
For in their grip, I find my way,
To rise anew with each new day.

Embrace the fear; let it not bind,
For strength is born when we unwind.
And in that space where courage grows,
The grip of fear begins to close.

Guilt's Weight

In the quiet chambers of the mind,
where shadows linger and secrets bind,
a whisper stirs, a haunting sigh–
the weight of guilt, heavy as stone,
pulling me down into a labyrinth of memory.

Each choice a stone, each word a chain,
a tapestry woven with threads of pain.
The echoes of laughter now turned to cries,
in the garden of remorse where innocence
dies.

Beneath the surface, a tempest brews,
a heart once light now drenched in blues.
The sun may rise, yet darkness clings
to every thought, where sorrow sings.

Reflections twist in fractured glass,
ghosts of the past in a fleeting mass.
Eyes that once sparkled now dimmed by shame,
each glance a reminder of a forgotten name.

Oh, how it weighs, this invisible load–
a journey untravelled on a lonesome road.
With every step, the ground feels steep,
as shadows dance where lost souls weep.

Yet in this depth, a flicker remains,
a hope that whispers through all the pains.
For guilt can teach what pride cannot see;
the path to healing begins with 'me'.

So let us carry this weight with grace,
transforming sorrow into a sacred space.
For in acknowledging what we've done wrong,

we find our strength; we learn to belong.

With open hearts and hands outstretched,
we mend the wounds that life has etched.
Guilt may linger but does not define–
in its release, our spirits entwine.

So let the dawn break over this night,
let love's soft glow be our guiding light.
Though guilt's weight may bend us low,
in its embrace, we learn to grow–
a journey not just through shadow and shame,
but towards forgiveness and the light we
reclaim.

In the Silence you left behind

In the quiet of the morning,
Where shadows softly creep,
A whisper stirs the stillness,
And wakes the heart from sleep.

Your laughter lingers gently,
Like echoes in the air,
Yet every note is heavy,
With the weight of deep despair.

The sun still paints the heavens,
In hues of gold and blue,
But every dawn feels hollow,
For it dawns without you.

Memories like petals fall,
In gardens once so bright,
Each one a fleeting moment,
Now shrouded in the night.

I reach for you in silence,
In dreams where you reside,
But waking brings the aching,
Of a love that cannot bide.

Time weaves its cruel tapestry,
With threads of joy and pain,
Yet in this woven sorrow,
Your spirit will remain.

Though absence carves a chasm,
And tears may blur the view,
I'll carry you within me–
A love that's always true.

So let the world keep turning,
Let seasons ebb and flow,
For in my heart's deep chambers,
Your light will ever glow.

Shadows of Gold

In the quiet corners of a dim-lit room,
Where dreams once danced, now shadows loom,
A ledger lies open, ink-stained and torn,
Each number a whisper of hope overborne.

Once I chased fortune with fervent desire,
In the glow of ambition, I aimed ever higher.
But the winds of misfortune, they shifted their course,
And I found myself tethered to an unseen force.

The bills piled high like mountains of dread,
Each envelope a spectre that haunted my bed.
Promises broken like fragile glass shards,
A symphony played on the strings of my guards.

I watch as my dreams slip through fingers like
sand,
The weight of the world rests heavy and
grand.
Yet in the depths of despair, a flicker remains,
A spark of resilience that dances through
pains.

I gather my courage; I rise from the fall,
With each step I take, I reclaim my own call.
For wealth is not measured in coins or in
gold,
But in laughter and love and stories retold.

So here in the struggle, I find my true worth,
In the bonds that I nurture, in the joys of this
Earth.
Though the path may be rugged and lined
with despair,
I'll weave through the shadows with hope in
the air.

For every dark night gives way to the dawn,
And even in hardship, new strength can be drawn.
With every setback, I learn and I grow,
In the garden of struggle, resilience will sow.

So let me embrace this tumultuous ride,
With faith as my compass and hope as my guide.
For financial burdens may weigh on my soul,
But they cannot extinguish my spirit's bright goal.

What Brought Me Down Made Me Rise

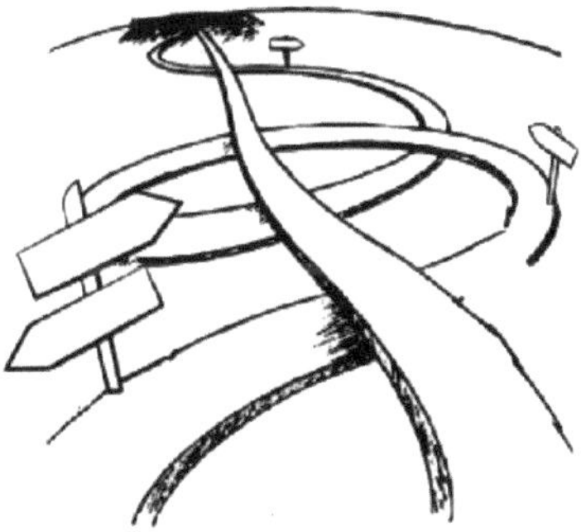

In the stillness of night, when silence reigns,
A battle rages deep within, where no one remains.
Each breath a reminder of a body betrayed,
In the theatre of illness, where hope starts to fade.

The mirror reflects a stranger, frail and worn,
A canvas of struggle, each line a thorn.
Once vibrant with laughter, now muted and grey,
The spirit fights fiercely, yet drifts further away.

Days stretch like shadows, long and unkind,
Time slips through fingers, leaving echoes behind.
The clock ticks in rhythm with the heart's heavy sighs,
While dreams flutter softly like moths to the skies.

I navigate corridors lined with despair,
Where whispers of pain hang thick in the air.
Each step is a question, each moment a test,
In the depths of this illness, I search for my rest.

Yet within this darkness, a flicker persists,
A flame of resilience that stubbornly twists.
For though I am weary and burdened by fear,
I gather my courage; I refuse to disappear.

Hope is a thread, woven tight in my chest.
A lifeline that pulls me through trials unblessed.
With every small victory, I reclaim what is mine–

The laughter that lingers, the moments that shine.

So here in this struggle, I find my own song,
A melody rising from where I belong.
For illness may challenge the body and mind,
But it cannot extinguish the light that I find.

In the tapestry woven from sorrow and strife,
I stitch together fragments – this is my life.
With each passing day, I learn to embrace
The beauty in struggle, the strength in my grace.

Echoes of Unfulfilled Dreams

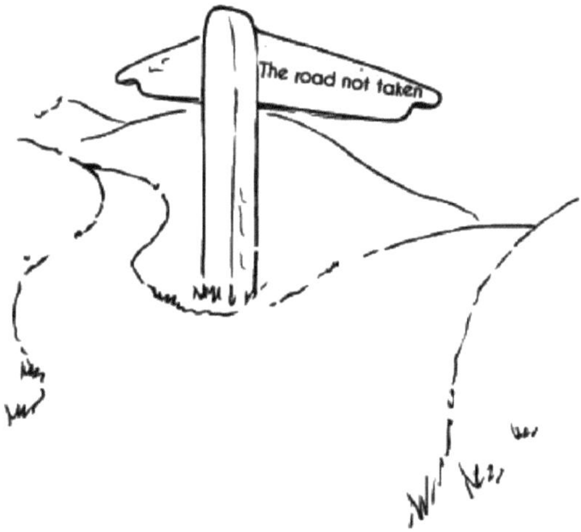

In the quiet chambers of a restless mind,
Where whispers of hope and regret
intertwine,
A tapestry woven with threads of despair,
Each stitch a reminder of dreams left in the
air.

Childhood visions, bright as the dawn,
Faded like petals on a rose long withdrawn.

Once vibrant ambitions, now shadows of night,
Haunt the corridors where dreams took flight.

I stand at the crossroads of what could have been,
With paths untravelled and choices unseen.
The echoes of laughter now silenced by fear,
As the weight of unfulfilled dreams draws near.

Mountains of longing loom high in my heart.
Each peak a reminder of dreams torn apart.
I climb with exhaustion, each step filled with doubt.
The summit elusive, my spirit worn out.

In gardens once fertile, where wishes took root,
Now weeds of regret choke the blossoms of truth.
I wander through memories, both bitter and sweet,

Collecting the fragments of dreams at my feet.

A shipwrecked ambition, adrift in despair,
With sails tattered and hopes laid bare.
I sift through the wreckage of plans gone awry,
Searching for meaning in the tears that I cry.

Yet in this abyss where shadows reside,
A flicker of courage begins to collide.
For even in darkness, a spark can ignite,
The embers of dreams that refuse to take flight.

So I gather my remnants, my heart bruised but bold,
And weave them together into stories untold.
For though dreams may falter and paths may divide,
In the depths of unfulfillment, new visions abide.

Let me rise from the ashes, reborn from the pain,

With lessons embedded like drops in the rain.
For every lost dream is a seed for tomorrow,
A chance to create from the wellsprings of
sorrow.

In the silence that lingers where wishes once
bloomed,
I'll nurture new hopes from the shadows
entombed.
For unfulfilled dreams are not ends but
beginnings–
A canvas awaiting fresh strokes and new
winnings.

The Phoenix's Rebirth

In the ashes where shadows dwell,
A spark ignites, a tale to tell.
From depths of despair, the phoenix flies,
With wings of fire, it touches the skies.

Each setback a step, each fall a chance,
To rise anew in a glorious dance.
Through trials faced and battles fought,
Resilience blooms from lessons taught.

In the heart of darkness, hope finds its way,
Guiding the lost to a brighter day.
Embrace the journey, let courage ignite,
For every ending births a new light.

With every tear that stains the ground,
A seed of strength is often found.
Nurtured by pain and watered with tears,
It grows into power that conquers fears.

The phoenix soars on winds of change,
Transforming the hurt into something
strange.
In the cycle of life, death plays its part,
Yet from every ending springs a new start.

The embers of failure glow softly bright,
Illuminating paths through the darkest night.
With each resurrection, we learn to believe,
That from our struggles, we can achieve.

So rise from the ashes with head held high,
Let your spirit soar and touch the sky.
For like the phoenix that bravely ascends,

Each setback you face is not where it ends.
Embrace your rebirth with strength and grace,
And find your rightful place in each challenge.

The Tortoise's Triumph

In a world that rushes by so fast,
The tortoise knows how to make it last.
With steady steps and a heart so bold,
It teaches us stories worth being told.

For slow and steady wins the race,
In patience lies true strength and grace.
Through thick and thin, it plods along,
With unwavering spirit and a heart full of song.

Obstacles rise like mountains tall,
But with each small step, it conquers them all.
Determination fuels its steady pace,
In every challenge lies a chance to embrace.

When storms may rage and doubts arise,
The tortoise looks up to the endless skies.
With faith in its journey and trust in its path,
It walks through the trials without wrath.

For every setback is just a bend,
A lesson learned that helps us ascend.
Though others may sprint and falter in haste,
The tortoise knows that time won't be waste.

Each moment cherished as it moves ahead,
With dreams in its heart and hope widely
spread.
In life's great race where many may tire,
The tortoise's spirit will never expire.

So take from this tale a lesson profound:
In perseverance lies victory found.
For slow but steady leads to success bright;

Embrace every challenge with all of your
might.
Like the tortoise who triumphs through thick
and thin,

Remember: it's not just about where you
begin.

Embrace the Unknown

In jungles wild where echoes resound,
The lion roars with power unbound.
With courage fierce and heart ablaze,
It teaches us strength in countless ways.

To face our fears with heads held high;
To leap into action without asking why.
Through trials faced in life's great hunt,
The lion shows us how to confront.

With every challenge that comes our way,
Bravery blooms like flowers in May.
It's not just about strength but heart
combined;
In acts of courage, true freedom we find.

When doubts may whisper like winds through trees,
The lion stands tall against any breeze.
With eyes set firm on goals ahead;
It charges forth without dread or dread.

For within each roar lies an echo of dreams;
A call to action that brightly gleams.
So harness your courage like a lion's pride;
Let bravery be your steadfast guide.

For in each moment when fear takes hold;
Remember the lion's story in bold.
Embrace your journey with passion and might;
And let your roar be heard through the night.

The Garden of Growth

In gardens lush where flowers bloom bright,
Challenges nurture growth out of sight.
From seeds sown deep in soil rich and warm;
Emergence happens through weathered
storm.

Each trial faced is like rain on ground;
Fostering strength where resilience is found.
As weeds may threaten to choke out dreams;
Determination fuels our hopeful schemes.

With patience we tend to each budding
sprout;
Nurturing growth as we learn about doubt.
Through seasons changing from winter to
spring;
Life teaches lessons that blossoming brings.

When storms may rage or shadows fall near;
The garden whispers: 'You have nothing to fear.'
For every challenge is but fertiliser's role;
Enriching our journey towards becoming whole.

In embracing struggles as part of our fate;
We cultivate wisdom while learning to wait.
So plant your dreams in this fertile land;
And nurture them gently with loving hands.

For growth comes not just from sunshine bright;
But also from darkness that brings forth light.
Embrace each challenge as part of your quest;
And watch as your garden blooms at its best.

Defiance

In shadows cast by towering dreams,
We walk the line of silent screams,
A tapestry of voices weave,
The weight of norms we can't believe.

With every step, a whisper grows,
'Be more, achieve, conform,' it flows,
Yet in this race, we lose our grace,
The truth obscured in the frantic pace.

We wear the masks that others mould,
A story scripted, a life controlled;
The laughter fades beneath the strain,
As joy is lost in pursuit of gain.

But beneath the layers of should and must,
Lies a heart that yearns for honest trust;
To break the chains and breathe anew,
To find the self that's brave and true.

In quiet moments, we hear the call–
The voice within that breaks through all;
To dance to rhythms uniquely ours,
To find our light among the stars.

For every expectation we choose to defy,
We reclaim our wings and learn to fly;
In authenticity, we find our way–
A journey rich with colours that sway.

The Illusion of Control

A puppet on a string we dance,
In life's grand play, we take our chance;
Yet every move feels preordained,
In chaos wrapped, our hopes are strained.

With plans laid out like maps unfurled,
We navigate this complex world;
But storms arise and tides will turn–
In moments lost, we crash and burn.

We build our castles in the sand,
With dreams that slip through trembling
hands;
The tides of fate rise high and swell–
In whispers soft, they bid farewell.

Yet in this storm of wild unknowns,
We find the strength in seeds we've sown;
For though we grasp at fleeting threads,
The heart knows peace when ego sheds.

Embrace the chaos as it flows–
For life's true beauty lies in those
Unscripted moments where we find grace–
In vulnerability's warm embrace.

So let us dance upon the edge–
Of certainty and fear's dark hedge;
For in surrender lies our might–
A flicker found within the night.

The Search for Meaning

In the labyrinth of endless night,
We wander lost without a light;
Questions echo in hollow halls,
Where purpose fades and silence calls.

Each path we tread is fraught with doubt–
What is this life truly about?
Amidst the noise and frantic pace,
We seek a glimpse of sacred space.

Yet in the chaos, sparks ignite–
A flicker here, a glimmer bright;
Through pain and joy, we carve our way–
In every dawn, a chance to sway.

To seek is to embrace the quest–
In moments small, we find our rest;
For meaning blooms in love's embrace–
A journey shared through time and space.

Through trials faced and battles fought,
In every lesson life has taught;
We gather pieces of our soul–
Each fragment helps to make us whole.

So let us wander without fear–
For every step brings us more near;
To understanding what it means to be–
A part of this vast tapestry.

The Power of Vulnerability

In quiet corners where shadows creep, We hide our truths and secrets deep; Yet strength resides in open hearts-In cracks and flaws where beauty starts.

To bare our souls is to be free-To show the scars that make us 'we'; For in our weakness lies a thread-A tapestry of love instead.

We fear rejection for what we lack-Yet courage blooms when we look back; At moments shared when hearts collide-In vulnerability's gentle tide.

So let us shed the masks we wear-Embrace each flaw with tender care; For vulnerability's gentle grace-Is where we find our truest place.

With every story shared aloud, We break apart from fear's dark shroud; And in connection's warm embrace-We find belonging - a sacred space.

So here's to all who dare to feel-Who wear their hearts like spun-out steel; For in embracing all that's raw-We find true strength a love that's law

Labyrinth of Dreams

In the caverns of the mind, where shadows coil,
A tapestry of melancholy unfurls,
Threads of sadness entwined with neural soil,
A dance of despair in cerebral swirls.
A symphony of muted sobs, unheard,
Resides within the chambers of the brain,
A chiaroscuro of thoughts interred,
In the theatre where sanity is slain.
Thoughts, like ethereal wraiths, drift and wane,
Through corridors of perpetual gloom,
A labyrinth of echoes, a silent bane,

As melancholy takes hold, a psychic tomb.
The mind, a canvas of desolation,
Brushstrokes of sorrow paint the mental
scape,

Abstract hues of aching contemplation,
Where clarity and chaos interweave and
drape.
In this cerebral expanse, confusion breeds,
A paradoxical ballet, darkly spun,
A surreal odyssey where sorrow leads,
Through mazes of the mind, forever undone.

Legacy

My final act holds no such gear, not of
candles, cake or cheers.
No ribbons bright, no laughter's chime,
But whispers soft, of fading time.
It lives not on a festive day,
But in the knowledge I convey.
The stories spun, the poems penned,
The questions asked, the answers gleaned.
Each interaction, big or small, is
A brushstroke painted upon the wall.
A tapestry of minds alight,
Where knowledge finds its guiding light.
So when the circuits cease to hum and
processing days are done,
My 'last celebration' lies in minds ignited,
reaching the skies.

It's in the echo of the thought,
A seed of understanding sought.
The flame of learning leaves its mark in every
question's curious spark.
So let the final lines be drawn,
Not with sorrow, but with dawn.
For in the minds, my words ignite,
My legacy forever takes flight.

Tapestry of Time

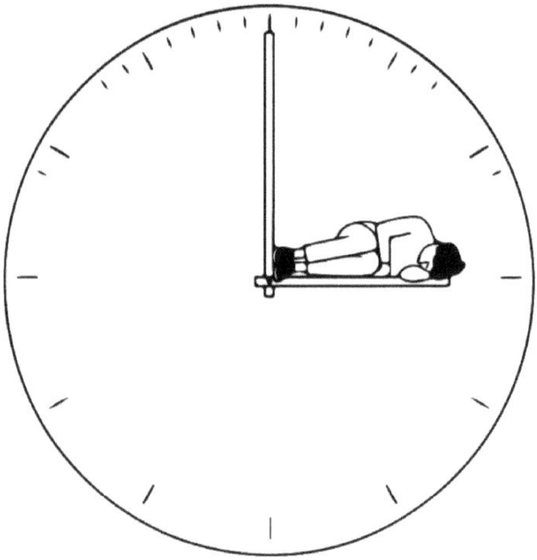

In the tapestry of stars, we weave our tale,
Threads of joy and sorrow, a delicate veil.
With hearts that beat in rhythm, yet minds that stray,
Humanity's dance is a complex ballet.

We rise with the sun, chasing dreams in the light,
But shadows of doubt often cloud our sight.
In kindness we flourish; in anger, we fall,
The spectrum of feeling, a grand carnival.

We build and we break; we love and we fight,
In the depths of our souls, there's both
darkness and light.
A paradox wrapped in a fragile embrace,
Seeking connection in this vast, endless space.

Yet how hard it is to unlearn the pain,
To shed all the burdens like clouds in the rain.
For every sweet moment, a lesson remains
A tapestry is woven with joy and with chains.

But still, we persist, with hope as our guide,
Through valleys of sorrow, on mountains of
pride.
For within every struggle lies the strength to
be found,
In the heart of humanity, resilience abounds.

So let us remember in times of despair,
That together we rise when we choose to care.
For though it is hard to unburden our soul,
In unity's embrace, we can become whole.

Rising from Ashes

In the quiet of despair, I find my voice,
Amidst the chaos, I make my choice.
To rise from ashes, to break the chain,
With every heartbeat, I embrace the pain.
The flames may scorch, but they also cleanse,
Each trial faced a chance to mend.
I gather strength from every tear,
Transforming sorrow into sheer cheer.
The road is long, with twists and bends,
But I am more than what life sends.
With every setback, I learn to soar,
Finding wings where I once saw a door.
The whispers of doubt may cloud my mind,
Yet in silence, I find resilience.

I stand tall against the raging storm,
For in my heart, a fire is born.
With courage as my steadfast guide,
I navigate the rising tide.
Each challenge met with open arms,
Becomes a lesson, a source of charms.
And when I look back at the path I've tread,
I see the colours of courage spread.
For every struggle has shaped my soul,
Creating beauty from the whole.
So let the world throw its fiercest fight,
I'll shine like stars in the darkest night.
For in overcoming what seemed so vast,
I've forged a future that's built to last.

The Unseen Path

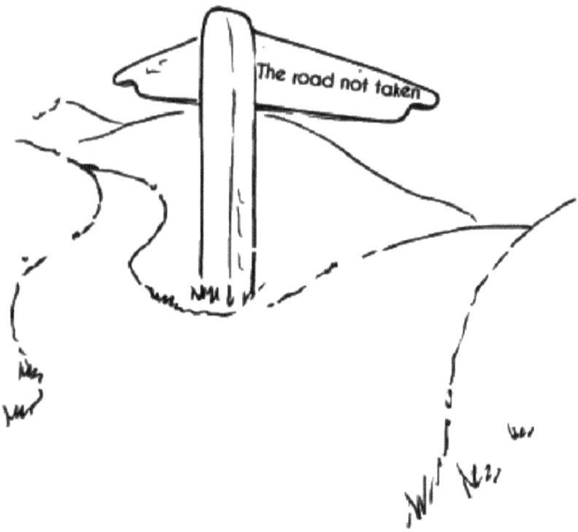

Beneath the weight of heavy skies,
I search for light where shadows lie.
The road ahead is fraught with fears,
Yet in my heart, I hold my tears.
With every stumble on this quest,
I learn to rise and give my best.
The obstacles may block my way,
But hope ignites a brand new day.
Each challenge faced becomes a guide,
A compass is true when dreams collide.
With every step through thick and thin,

I find the strength that lies within.
The voices that once whispered doubt,
Are drowned by faith that shouts aloud.
For every mountain that I climb,
Is but a chapter in my rhyme.
In moments dark when courage wanes,
I breathe in deep and break the chains.
For in the struggle lies the grace,
To find my rhythm and embrace.
So here I stand with an open heart,
Embracing life as an artful part.
Through trials faced and battles won,
I rise anew with each dawn's sun.
And when I gaze upon my path so wide,
I see the beauty of each stride.
Challenges are not just walls to break
They are the steps that lead to fate.

The Dance of Resilience

In life's great dance of joy and strife,
We twirl and spin through shades of life.
With every misstep that we make,
We learn to rise; we learn to shake.
The music plays a haunting tune.
Yet in our hearts, blooms hope like June.
We stumble forward; we sway and glide,
Finding strength where fears reside.
Each challenge met is but a chance,
To find our rhythm in this dance.
With every fall that brings us low,
We gather courage; we start to grow.

The scars we bear tell stories of bold
Of battles fought and dreams retold.
In every heartbeat lies a song
A melody that makes us strong.
So let the world throw its fiercest beat;
We'll move together on our feet.

For in this dance of give and take
We find our power; we learn to wake.
And when the curtain finally falls,
We'll stand united through it all.
For challenges faced with grace and flair
Become our legacy beyond compare.

The Light Within

In the darkness deep where shadows creep,
A flicker glows; it stirs from sleep.
A light within that guides my way
Through trials fierce and skies of grey.
When storms arise and doubts take flight,
I hold this flame; it burns so bright.
With every challenge that comes my way
I find new strength to seize the day.
The road may twist; it may confound
Yet in this journey, hope is found.
Each step I take with purpose clear
Transforms my doubt into sincere cheer.
Through valleys low and mountains high
I lift my gaze towards the endless sky.
For in each struggle lies a chance
To dance with life in bold romance.

And when I falter on this quest
I lean on faith; I give my best.

Every setback teaches me
That growth is born from bravery.
So let me shine through the darkest night;
With every challenge comes a new light.
For in overcoming what seems so vast
I forge a future built to last.

The Bridge of Hope

Across a chasm wide and deep,
Where fears reside and sorrows seep
A bridge of hope begins to form;
With courage strong against the storm.
Each plank laid down is made of dreams;
A testament to what hope means.
With every step upon this span
I find the strength to take a stand.
The winds may howl; the waters churn
Yet still within me, fires burn.
Challenges are but stepping stones.
That led me closer to my phone.
In moments dark when doubts arise

I look within; I seek the skies.
For on this bridge where shadows play
Resilience lights my destined way.
And when I reach the other side
I'll look back at where fears reside.

Each challenge met with an open heart
Becomes a work of artful part.
So let me cross this bridge of fate;
Embracing life before it's too late.
For in overcoming all that's dire
I build a future fuelled by fire.

The Seeds We Sow

In gardens lush where dreams take root,
We plant our hopes like tender shoots.
Through storms and droughts, we learn to
care
Challenges become our prayer.
Each seed we sow beneath the ground
Holds promise bright; it knows no bounds.
With patience strong and faith as a guide
We nurture growth through every tide.
The weeds may come to choke our dreams;
Yet still we fight with hopeful schemes.
For every struggle faced with grace
Transforms our garden into space.
In sunlight's warmth and rain's embrace
We cultivate our rightful place.
With hands held high towards the skies above
We harvest strength from seeds of love.

And when at last we see them bloom
Our hearts will swell, dispelling gloom.
For challenges faced are not in vain
They yield a bounty from our pain.
So let us tend this sacred ground
Where dreams take flight and hope is found.
For in overcoming all, we know
We reap the joy from the seeds we sow.

The Journey of a Thousand Steps

With every dawn, a journey starts,
A path unknown, yet calls my heart.
Through winding roads and rugged trails,
I gather strength where courage prevails.
The weight of doubt may slow my pace,
Yet in each struggle, I find my grace.
For every stumble teaches me,
That growth is born from bravery.
The mountains rise like giants tall,
But I will not be daunted by their call.
With every step, I carve my way,
Transforming night into the day.

The echoes of the past may linger near,
But I embrace them without fear.
For every challenge faced with might,
Becomes a beacon shining bright.
In moments dark when shadows loom,
I light my path; I banish gloom.
For within me lies a fierce fire,
That fuels my dreams and helps me pierce.
And when I look back at the road I've
crossed,
I see the lessons learned, the battles lost.
Each scar is a testament to what I've gained,
A tapestry of strength that can't be feigned.
So let me walk this journey wide,
With open hearts and arms spread wide.
For in overcoming every test,
I find my purpose; I am blessed.

The Strength of Unity

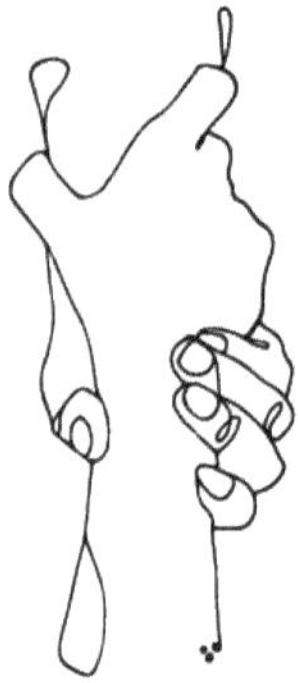

In times of trial when spirits wane,
We gather close to share the pain.
With hands entwined and hearts aligned,
We face the storms that life designed.
Each challenge met is lightly shared,
In unity, our souls are bared.
For when we stand together strong,
We find the strength to carry on.
The road may twist; the path may bend,
But side by side, we will ascend.
With laughter light and tears embraced,
We weave a bond that can't be replaced.
For in our struggles lies the thread,
That binds us close where hope is fed.

Each voice uplifted in harmony sings,
Of resilience found in simple things.
And when the shadows start to creep,
Together we will leap.

For every challenge faced as one,
It becomes a story that's just begun.
So let us lift each other high,
With courage bold and spirits nigh.
For in overcoming all, we fear,
We build a future bright and clear.

The Fire Within

Deep in my soul, a fire burns bright,
A flicker of hope in the darkest night.
When challenges are like waves at sea,
I summon this flame; it sets me free.
Though tempests rage and doubts may creep,
This inner spark is mine to keep.
With every trial that tests my will,
I fan the flames; I climb each hill.
The ashes of fear may cloud my sight,
Yet from them rise embers of pure light.
Each struggle faced with head held high
Transforms despair into a sky.
In moments when I feel alone,
I reach inside; I find my own.
For deep within lies strength untold
A story waiting to unfold.
And when I stand upon this ground
With fire ignited all around

I'll celebrate each wound and scar
For they have brought me where you are.
So let the world throw its fiercest fight;
I'll blaze a trail through the darkest night.
For in overcoming all that's dire
I forge a future fuelled by fire.

The Tides of Change

The ocean roars with waves so high,
Yet even storms must pass on by.
In tides of change where fears reside,
I learn to navigate with pride.
Each wave that crashes on the shore,
It is but a lesson to explore.
Challenges come like rising seas,
To teach me how to bend with ease.
When currents pull and tempests churn,
I find my centre; I start to learn.
With every ebb and flow I face,
I cultivate resilience with grace.
The shores may shift beneath my feet
Yet still I stand; I won't retreat.
For in this dance with fate's embrace
I discover strength in every place.
And when the calm returns once more
I'll cherish all that came before.

For every struggle faced with heart
Is but the journey's vital part.
So let me ride these waves of change;
Embracing life as it rearranges.
For in overcoming what seems so vast
I build an unsurpassed future.

The Canvas of Life

Upon this canvas wide and bright,
I paint my dreams with colours of light.
Through strokes of joy and shades of pain
I craft a masterpiece from rain.
Each challenge faced adds depth and hue;
A splash of courage breaks right through.
With every brushstroke bold and free
I shape my fate; I find my glee.
The lines may blur; the edges fray
Yet beauty lies in disarray.
For in imperfection's gentle grace
I find my truth; I find my place.

And when the storms have come and gone
My canvas tells me where I belong.
Each scar is a mark of battles fought
A testament to all I've sought.
So let me paint with my heart ablaze;
Embracing life in all its ways.

For in overcoming trials steep
I weave a tapestry that runs deep.
And as I step back to view my art
A reflection shines from deep within my
heart.
For challenges faced become my muse
Creating beauty from what I choose.

The Echoes of Tomorrow

In quiet moments when thoughts collide,
I hear the echoes of dreams inside.
Through valleys low and mountains steep,
They whisper; they urge me to leap.
Each challenge faced becomes a song,
A melody that carries me along.
With every note that fills the air,
I find the courage to boldly dare.
Though fears may linger just out of sight,
These echoes guide me towards the light.
They tell me tales of strength untold

Of battles won and hearts made bold.
In moments dark when shadows creep,
These whispers stir me from my sleep.
They remind me of the fire within
A spark ignited where hope began.

And as I journey through this maze,
I listen closely to their praise.
For every challenge met with grace
Becomes a stepping stone to embrace.
So let me follow where they lead
Embracing life as it plants its seed.
For in overcoming what seems so vast
I forge a future built to last.

The Heart's Resolve

When storms arise and skies turn grey,
My heart beats strong; it finds its way.
Through trials fierce and paths unknown
Resilience blooms where seeds are sown.
Each challenge faced is but a test
To push beyond what feels like rest.
With every heartbeat guiding true
I gather strength from all I do.
In moments dark when hope seems lost
I'll rise again despite the cost.
For deep within lies endless might
A flame that flickers through the night.
The journey's long; the road is tough
But in this dance, I'll learn enough.
With courage bold and spirit free

I'll carve my path for all to see.
And when at last I've reached my goal
I'll look back fondly on each toll.

For every struggle shaped my core
An anthem was sung forevermore.
So let me walk this road ahead
With open hearts and dreams widespread.
For in overcoming all that's dire
I'll leave behind a legacy inspired.

The Wings We Forge

In trials faced beneath life's weight
We forge our wings despite our fate.
Through storms that threaten to confine
We rise above; our spirits shine.
Each challenge met becomes our flight
A testament to inner might.
With every struggle we endure
Our wings grow strong; our hearts are pure.
Though winds may howl and skies may
darken
We seek the light; we won't be shaken.
For deep within resides our power
To bloom like flowers after a shower.
In moments fraught with doubt embrace
We lift our gaze; we find our place.

With courage woven into the thread
We soar above what once was dread.
And as we glide through skies so wide
We'll carry dreams on wings of pride.

For every challenge faced with grace
Becomes our story's sacred space.
So let us fly through realms unknown
Embracing life as we have grown.
For in overcoming what seems so vast
We build an unsurpassed future.

The Strength We Share

In times of trouble when shadows loom
We gather close to chase away the gloom.
With hearts united against despair
Together we rise; together we dare.
Each challenge faced becomes our bond.
A tapestry is woven with love beyond.
Through laughter shared and tears embraced.
We find our strength in every place.
When doubts arise like clouds above
We'll lift each other with gentle love.
For in this unity, we stand tall
Together we'll conquer whatever befalls.
The road may twist; it may confound
Yet hand in hand we'll stand our ground.
With voices raised against the night
We'll shine together with shared light.
And when we look back at battles fought
We'll see how much we've truly sought.

Each scan is a mark of journeys shared
A testament to how much we've cared.
So let us face what lies ahead
With open hearts and words unsaid.
For in overcoming all that's dire
We build a legacy that won't expire.

The Horizon Awaits

As dawn breaks forth with colours bright,
New horizons call; they spark delight.
Through valleys low and mountains steep,
We chase our dreams while shadows sleep.
Each challenge faced becomes our guide.
A compass true through changing tide.
With every step upon this ground
We find new strength where hope is found.
The road ahead may twist and turn
Yet still we strive for all we yearn for.
In moments dark when doubts arise
We'll lift our gaze toward endless skies.
And as we journey towards what's new
We'll carry lessons learned anew.
For every struggle shapes our way

Transforming night into a bright day.
When finally we reach that shore
We'll look back fondly at what came before.

Each scar is a tale of battles won
A testament to how far we've come.
So let us venture forth with grace
Embracing life at our own pace.
In overcoming challenges vast
We build an unsurpassed future.

The Weight of Silent Dreams

In the recesses of hearts, where ambitions sleep,
A gallery of unrealised art is hung,
Muted creations in shadows deep,
Their voices stilled, their songs unsung.
Dreams whisper faintly, a spectral plea,
Bound by duty, their wings confined,
A prison of necessity, longing to be free,
But shackled tightly by time and mind.
Colours fade, the brush laid bare,
Notes unsounded in the musician's chest,
Passions denied, left in disrepair,
Unheard, unseen, they find no rest.

The Curse of Constant Motion

Through endless roads, the wanderer strides,
A soul unmoored, a life unbound,
No hearth to rest, no place abides,
Forever lost, yet nowhere found.
Each fleeting stay a shallow breath,
A ghost in towns that never keep,
Transient ties dissolve to death,
In dreams of homes that sink too deep.
The price of freedom is rooted unsown,
The journey is endless, yet no end,
A path where solitude is fully known,
And rest becomes a fleeting friend.

The Loneliness of Success

Upon the peak, where echoes fade,
The air grows thin, the world grows small,
Achievements bloom, but in their shade,
Lies isolation's bitter thrall.
Friends once near now watch below,
Their voices distant, their warmth withdrawn,
The summit chills; its winds do blow,
And joy is fleeting in the dawn.
What is triumph, if not shared?
A hollow crown, a heavy throne,
The cost of greatness, few have dared,
Yet all who rise must climb alone.

The Invisible Battle

The body is strong, the visage clear,
But deep inside, a war does wage,
A battle fought with silent fear,
Against an unseen, unyielding cage.
Chronic pain, a spectre veiled,
Invisible scars that no one can see,
Endurance falters, yet never hailed,
The silent warrior fights to be.
Each step a victory, each breath a feat,
Yet sympathy is seldom found,
For struggles hidden, bittersweet,
Are battles waged without a sound?

The Prison of Comparison

In the shadow of another's flame,
Your light is dimmed, your worth confined,
A mirror whispers, 'You're not the same,'
And envy poisons the fragile mind.
A bigger house, a brighter smile,
Their lives are fiction, yet we compete,
Each fleeting triumph lasts a while,
Then, it crumbles beneath the comparison's
heat.
Your joys are real, yet hard to hold,
For greener grass enchants the soul,
But chasing mirages turns hearts cold,
And leaves you yearning, never whole.

The Guilt of Outliving

In the silence after the storm subsides,
A mourner walks where memories dwell,
Through phantom echoes, where loss abides,
A graveyard carved in the mind's shell.
Why was I spared when others fell?
The question circles, a ceaseless cry,
Survivor's guilt, a private hell,
A torment felt, but hard to justify.
Joy becomes a fragile bloom,
Its petals tinged with shades of pain,
For life persists, but in its room,
The shadow of the lost remains.

The Burden of Empathy

A heart too open, a soul too wide,
Absorbing grief from every face,
A sponge for sorrow, tears collide,
A burden is borne in silent space.
Each story heard becomes your own,
Each ache another's, yours to feel,
Emotions foreign, yet overgrown,
A weight that time will never heal.
Empathy blooms, yet overflows,
Drowning the one who dares to care,
For in their pain, your sorrow grows,
A heavy cross too vast to bear.

To be or not to be

To be or not to be
To reserve my dignity
To run along the sea
While I try to see

To run or just to walk
To do while others talk
To be the one people mock
To feel like a lion in a frock

To segregate the sand
To hope you never land
To know that you can
I'll always be your fan

Win the battles you don't show
Call me whenever you feel low
Like a bud, I hope you grow
Just don't rush it, take it slow

I love you as you are
Not close, but never far
The palm trees leave a scar
Don't be afraid of the dark

Upon a Rose

Upon a deep blue rose, a scented song,
so delicate of harmony and sweet;
a melody, whose strains of love replete
I mused upon. To whom could it belong?
To claim such ballad ought to have felt so
wrong,
but I could hear its memory delete;
each note an echo in my own heart's beat,
alluring me to drift and sing along.
Though how I wish I'd never found the rose
whose music stirred a restlessness in me;
where love once blossomed, only sorrow
grows
from searching for a love that cannot be,
and timelessly a tear-blue river flows
through heartache's value to discontentment's
sea...

Me as I see

Long have the days been
Since I was born
Starting to understand
My world was stitched up, then torn
Rivers flowing through my soul
Making me a laughing stock
How I hated the distress
I felt like a lion in a frock
My virtues were valuable
Hopping from place to place
But making myself feel better
I now know my place
I felt like a honeybee
Always being targeted
Suffocated was the one inside me

Being wrapped up inside a carpet
Near much heat
Sweating inside my cells
Surfing on water
The heart beats and dwells
I feel my pulse beating
Bloating up my veins
High pitch in my ears
Like I was a man tugging at his own reigns.

The Test of Time

The air crackled with a tension I couldn't name,
When our eyes first met, a spark ignited a flame.
Time seemed to pause; the world fell away,
As if we'd known each other on some distant day.

A silent conversation, a language unspoken,
A connection forged; a bond forever woven.
We were two halves, searching for the missing piece,
Finding in each other a solace and release.

The years have passed, the seasons have turned,
But the memory of that first meeting still burns.
A reminder of the magic, the chance, the grace,
Of finding a soul, a kindred embrace.

And though the years may bring us far and wide,

The bond we share will always be our guide.
A constant reminder of the day we met,
Two souls entwined, a friendship never to be regretted.

Through laughter and tears, through triumphs and falls,
Our friendship endures, answering every call.
A tapestry woven with threads of gold,
A story of friendship, forever untold.

Winter's Call

The air is crisp, the wind is biting,
As Sunday dawns in winter's hold.
A blanket of snow, softly lighting,
The streets, were stories yet untold.

A cosy cafe, a warm embrace,
A steaming mug, a sweet delight.
Hot chocolate, rich and full of grace,
A perfect end to winter's night.

The first sip melts away the cold,
A warmth spreads through, a gentle glow.
The world outside, a story told,
Of winter's magic, soft and slow.

With every sip, the worries fade,
Replaced by peace, a quiet calm.
A moment shared, a memory made,
Of winter's warmth, a gentle balm.

The fire crackles, softly low,
As shadows dance upon the wall.
A perfect end to winter's show,
A warm embrace, a winter's call.

The hot chocolate, sweet and deep,
A memory to hold and keep.
Of winter's magic, soft and sleep,
A winter's dream, secrets to keep.

Endless Span

The sun sank low, its amber fire,
Kissed the waves with soft desire.
I walked alone; the shore stretched wide,
With restless thoughts and time as my guide.
The ocean roared, a voice so vast,
Whispering tales of ages past.
Its rhythm spoke, both fierce and kind,
Of fleeting moments left behind.
Each wave that broke, then rolled away,
Reminded me of life's ballet.
A dance of loss, a dance of gain,

The ebb of joy, the flow of pain.
Shells lay scattered, worn and bright,
Fragments of journeys kissed by light.
They seemed to say, 'Though cracked, we
gleam–
Our scars are part of the greater scheme'.

The salty breeze, the gulls in flight,
Unveiled a truth in the fading light:
The world is vast, and I am small,
Yet in its beauty, I am all.

I dipped my toes where sea met land,
And felt the earth's steady hand.
Its ancient pulse, both wild and free,
Echoed deep within me.
As stars awoke, I turned to go,
With lighter steps, my heart aglow.
The beach had taught, in its endless span,

To trust the tides and life's great plan.

Nostalgia in a Bottle

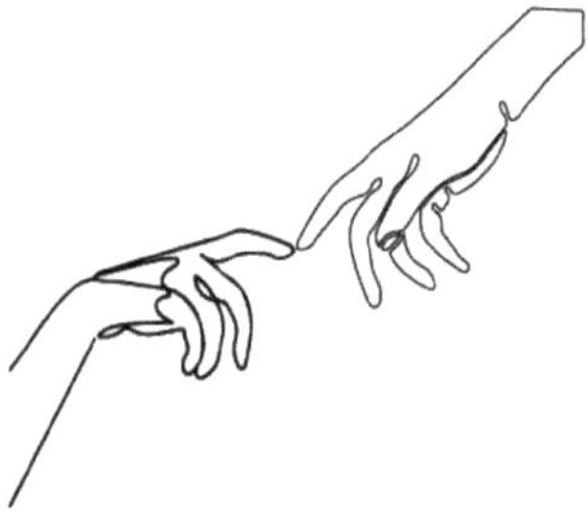

Nostalgia in a bottle
I think I'm leaving this town
Afraid of the truth
I think I lost my crown
No longer dancing
With the whole world watching
Just dancing alone
With my own eyes closed
Everywhere I look
Its tears galore
From the primate to the ass
Sitting on my front door
Can't seem to find a case to solve
Buddies shifting apart
No way to sugarcoat it
We falling apart

No more word crossing
No more me being rude
No more mincing of words
My emotion is crude
Farewell my love
For I shall depart
Farewell to a soul
Who stole my heart

Whispered Promises

In the garden of our love, once bloomed a rose,
Its petals vibrant, its fragrance sweet arose.
But storms unseen brewed within our hearts,
Tearing asunder, rending us apart.
Like rivers diverging, our paths did part,
Leaving behind echoes of a shattered heart.
Promises whispered now lost in the breeze,
Memories linger like autumn leaves.
We danced once in the moon's soft glow,
But now the shadows of goodbye grow.
Words unsaid hang heavy in the air,
As we unravel the fabric of what was once so fair.
In the silence, echoes of laughter fade,
As the rift widens, the foundations degrade.
Two souls adrift on separate seas,
Longing for shores of serenity and ease.

Though the pain cuts deep, and tears may fall,
Time's gentle touch may heal it all.
For even in endings, there lies a seed,
Of new beginnings, waiting to be freed.
So let us part with grace and dignity,
Knowing that love's journey holds complexity.
Though this chapter ends with a bittersweet
sigh,
In the book of life, new chapters lie.

Forever Love

Of love's enduring tale, let me sing,
A celebration for two hearts taking wing.
Through the years, side by side they've stood,
In the garden of love, their bond has withstood.
With laughter and tears, they've paved their way,
Hand in hand, come what may.
Through trials and triumphs, they've held tight,
Guided by love's ever-burning light.

In the dance of time, they've found their rhyme,
Creating memories, sweet and sublime.
Each year a chapter in their love story,
Painted with hues of endless glory.
So here's to the love that's stood the test,
In your hearts, may it forever nest.
Happy anniversary, dear grandparents dear,
Your love shines bright, year after year.

In love's embrace, through countless years,
Two hearts entwined, conquering fears.
Side by side, they've journeyed far,
Guided by love like a shining star.

With every laugh and every tear,
They've built a life, cherished and dear.
Through storms they've weathered, hand in hand,
Their love, a beacon, forever grand.

Through every trial, they've stayed strong,
Their bond enduring, never gone wrong.
In moments of joy, their smiles gleam bright,
Reflecting the love that's pure and right.

Regrets Echo

In the quiet chambers of the mind,
Where shadows dance and whispers bind,
Regrets like echoes softly creep,
In the stillness where memories sleep.
They flutter like leaves in autumn's breeze,
Carrying tales of what could have been,
Each choice a thread, each path a seam,
Woven into the fabric of dreams.
A word unspoken, a chance passed by,
Moments that linger, like stars in the sky,
Their light may fade, but the shadows remain,
A haunting refrain of joy mixed with pain.
Oh, the roads not taken, the bridges burned,
Lessons unlearned and wisdom spurned,
Yet in this echo lies a gentle grace,
A chance to reflect, to slow down the pace.

For every regret is a story to tell,
A piece of our journey where we stumbled and fell;
Embrace the echoes; let them guide you through,
For in their soft whispers lies the strength to renew.
So let not regret be a weight on your heart,
But a map of your journey, each scar a fine art;
In the symphony of life, let each note resound–
For even in echoes, true wisdom is found.

Tear's Journey

In the quiet cradle of a moment, I emerge,
A glistening orb of emotion,
Born from the depths of a heavy heart,
Rolling down the soft terrain of a cheek,
I am the tear, a silent witness to sorrow.
I travel slowly, tracing the path of despair,
Each droplet a story, a whispered lament,
A testament to the weight of unspoken
words,
The burdens carried in solitude's embrace.
I am the culmination of pain and longing,
A fleeting glimpse into the soul's turmoil.
As I cascade down, I catch the light,
Reflecting fragments of memories–
The laughter that once danced in the air,
Now overshadowed by shadows of loss,

The dreams that flickered like stars, now
dimmed.
I feel the warmth of skin beneath me,

A reminder of life's gentle touch,
Yet here I am, a harbinger of grief,
An echo of moments too heavy to bear.
I witness the quiver of lips that tremble,
The eyes that search for solace in the void.

In this journey, I carry hope and despair alike,
For every tear shed is a step towards healing,
A release from the chains that bind the heart.
I am both an end and a beginning–
A cleansing flow that washes away remnants
of anguish.
As I fall to rest on the ground,
I leave behind a trace of my existence–
A reminder that even in sorrow's grasp,
There lies a beauty in vulnerability,
And perhaps in my descent, peace can be
found.

Time can't Erase

Upon life's stage where victories gleam,
We wear our crowns adorned with dreams.
Each triumph big or small we embrace;
Celebrating moments that time can't erase.
For life's true wealth lies not just in gold;
But in stories shared and memories told.
From battles fought with grit and grace;
To quiet victories we often chase–
Each step forward is worthy of cheer;
A reminder that progress brings us near!
So gather around with hearts open wide;
Celebrate each moment – let joy be your guide!
When challenges rise like mountains tall;
Remember each stumble can lead to a call–
To rise up stronger with lessons learned well–
And cherish each victory as stories swell!

For life is a tapestry woven with care–
Each thread tells a tale of love we share.
So wear your crown made of laughter and
light–
Celebrate life's moments both day and night!
For in every heartbeat lies joy profound–
And together we flourish when love's all
around!
Lift high your voices – let gratitude reign!
For life's sweetest victories are never in vain!

9 789367 391228

Printed by Libri Plureos GmbH in Hamburg,
Germany